AF092307

Deathly Hallows Notebook by Hale Magick

Copyright © 2019 by InfinitYou

Cover Design by InfinitYou

ISBN 978-3-7497-7198-1 (Paperback)

All rights reserved. No part of this book may be reproduced without written permission of the copyright owner, except for the use of limited quotations for the purpose of book reviews.

This journal belongs to

_____

_____

_____

"Things we lose have a way of coming back to us in the end, if not always in the way we expect." - Luna Lovegood.

Simple To Do Checklist

○ _____

○ _____

○ _____

○ _____

○ _____

○ _____

○ _____

○ _____

○ _____

○ _____

○ _____

○ _____

○ _____

○ _____

○ _____

www.ingramcontent.com/pod-product-compliance
Lightning Source LLC
LaVergne TN
LVHW060327080526
838202LV00053B/4433